THE
HOUSE KEEPER

by Morna Regan

The House Keeper

by Morna Regan

The House Keeper was first performed at Project Arts Centre, Dublin on 24 April 2012. The cast, creative team and production team were as follows:

Mary	**Cathy Belton**
Beth	**Ingrid Craigie**
Hal	**Robert O'Mahoney**

Director	**Lynne Parker**
Set & Costume Designer	**Bláithín Sheerin**
Lighting Designer	**Sarah Jane Shiels**
Dramaturg	**Maureen White**
Assistant Director	**Rosemary McKenna (SEEDS Programme)**

Production Manager	**Rob Furey**
Stage Director	**Diarmuid O'Quigley**
Stage Manager	**Stephanie Ryan**
Hair & Make-Up	**Val Sherlock**
Production Electrician	**Adam Fitzsimons**
Set Construction	**Ian Thompson**
Scenic Artist	**Sandra Butler**

Graphic Design	**Detail Design Studio**
Photography	**Pat Redmond**
PR	**Gerry Lundberg PR**
Intern	**Sinéad Kearns**
Company Manager	**Justin Murphy**
Producers	**Diego Fasciati**
	Clare Robertson

The House Keeper was developed from a short play by Morna Regan commissioned by Origin Theatre Company, New York, for *End of Lines* as part of 1st Irish 2008, New York's annual festival of Irish theatre. To learn more about Origin Theatre and 1st Irish visit
www.origintheatre.org

Morna Regan

Morna Regan is from Derry City, Northern Ireland, and is currently living in London. She studied English and Drama at the University of London and Central School of Speech and Drama and received a Fulbright Scholarship to undertake an MFA in Theatre at the University of Southern California, Los Angeles. She worked as an actor for many years before starting to write, performing with such companies as Rough Magic Theatre Company, the Abbey Theatre, the Gate Theatre and various UK and US companies.

Morna's short film *The Case of Majella McGinty* was directed by Kirsten Sheridan in 2000 and and received festival awards at Foyle, Cork, San Francisco, Cologne, and Worldfest Houston. It was also nominated for Best Short Film at the Irish Film and Television Awards.

Morna's first play, *Midden*, was originally produced by Rough Magic Theatre Company and directed by Lynne Parker at the Traverse Theatre, Edinburgh, Hampstead Theatre, London, and on an Irish Tour. It was the recipient of an Edinburgh Fringe First Award in 2001, the Stewart Parker Radio Play Award, the Jayne Snow Award at the Dublin Theatre Festival, an Irish Times/ESB Theatre Awards Nomination and the Heidelberg European Author's Award. Morna has recently completed her first feature-length screenplay, *Away from the Sun,* with Writer's Only Funding from the Irish Film Board.

Rough Magic Theatre Company was founded in 1984 and has established itself as one of the leading independent theatre companies in Ireland. Based in Dublin, the company regularly performs at Project Arts Centre and tours in Ireland, the UK and beyond, garnering many awards, both at home and abroad.

Since its foundation, Rough Magic has built an organisation based on three core values: artistic excellence, an egalitarian approach to the creative ensemble and an ethic based on pluralism. The company has evolved around the principle that we are part of a world culture that can celebrate Irish identity diverse in its nature and outward-looking in its vision.

Rough Magic is committed to commissioning new Irish work for the stage, presenting the best of contemporary international writing and innovative productions from the classical repertoire. Frequently we use music as a transformative agent in live performance. The company's broad spectrum of work includes over forty Irish premieres and the debuts of many Irish theatre-makers.

In addition, we are active in the development of new theatre artists. Our pioneering SEEDS programme is now the benchmark for professional development in Irish theatre and the only one of its kind. In 2011 we launched a parallel programme for established artists, ADVANCE. Rough Magic is an enabler for the work of many individual artists and emerging companies, through mentoring, resource-sharing and production and administrative support.

Through these strategic initiatives, the richness of its artistic ambition and its national and international reach, Rough Magic is connected across the full spectrum of theatre activity, experience and creative practice. With each project we undertake, the aim is firstly to make great theatre, but also to advance and contribute to the cultural life of Ireland.

Rough Magic Theatre Company
18 South Great George's Street Dublin 2 Ireland
tel: +353 (0) 1 671 9278 email: info@roughmagic.ie web: www.roughmagic.ie
Registered Number: 122753

ROUGH MAGIC

Rough Magic Theatre Company

Artistic Director	**Lynne Parker**
Executive Producer	**Diego Fasciati**
Producer/Artist Development	**Clare Robertson**
Company Manager	**Justin Murphy**
Dramaturg	**Maureen White**
Associate Directors	**Sophie Motley**
	Matt Torney
Accountant	**Katy Falkingham**
Intern	**Sinéad Kearns**

Board of Directors
Marie Redmond (Chair)
Paul Brady
Anne Fogarty
Roy Foster
Darragh Kelly
Stephen McManus
Sheila O'Donnell
Gerry Smyth

Advisory Council
Siobhán Bourke
Anne Byrne
Catherine Donnelly
Declan Hughes
Darragh Kelly
Pauline McLynn
Hélène Montague
Martin Murphy
Arthur Riordan
Stanley Townsend

ADVANCE Artists
Denis Clohessy
Annabelle Comyn
Peter Daly
Rob Furey

SEEDS Artists
Zia Holly
Rosemary McKenna
Ronan Phelan
Matt Smyth
Hugh Travers

**Rough Magic gratefully acknowledges the support of the Arts Council/
An Comhairle Ealaíon, our patrons and Dublin City Council.**

THE HOUSE KEEPER

Morna Regan

Acknowledgements

For their support in the writing of this play I would like to thank
Sara Barnes, Franki Calouri, Alastair Galbraith, Mercy Hooper,
Lynne Parker and everyone at Rough Magic Theatre Company,
Tim Crouch, Rebecca Lenkiewicz and the Arvon Foundation,
George Heslin, Aoife Regan, Darragh Kelly, Gina Moxley,
Hilary O'Shaughnessy, Annie Siddons, Lisa Foster and Harriet
Pennington Legh at Alan Brodie Representation, The Tyrone
Guthrie Centre, and Matt and Mary Regan.

M.R.

For Nancy and Maeve

Love always

4

Characters

MARY, *late thirties – early forties*
BETH, *sixties*
HAL, *older*

The play is set in Manhattan in the present day.

Note on Text

Leon Scallick's Disease is a fictional genetic disorder affecting Hal's motor function, and is at the early stages of impairing his cognitive ability.

A dash followed by an ellipsis (– …) indicates a word is lost and momentarily searched for.

This text went to press before the end of rehearsals and so may differ slightly from the play as performed.

It is the middle of the night in a large, masculine room, in a rundown brownstone mansion. The decor appears untouched for decades, although it is obvious that a lot of money was spent on it at one time. A musty Persian rug takes up most of the floor space. Stage right houses a formidable partners desk. Stage left recesses to a large window downstage of which two leather wingback chairs and a standing lamp gather round a small table.

These original furnishings now share the room with piles of broken, more modern and incongruous furniture, and other household detritus. The desk resides under such a pile.

MARY, *preset, is going at the rug with an old-fashioned carpet sweeper, which demands her full weight. It isn't working very well so she flips it over and starts pulling at the skeins of hair and lint clogging it.*

Holding the entrails at arm's length, she dumps them in an empty box.

On her way back she goes to the window, scrapes some grime off to see out, and checks below. She pauses a moment, then goes at the carpet again with renewed purpose.

Beat.

The door begins to open slowly, spilling some landing light, which illuminates BETH, *unseen by* MARY.

She is wearing plain pyjamas and a pair of oversized brown-leather sandals. Despite this, and years of personal neglect, the assurance of moneyed breeding is still very much to the fore in BETH's *bearing.*

She watches MARY *a moment then slowly raises her arm, bringing a hammer into view. She studies her mark until* MARY *senses her and turns.*

MARY. Oh! Edith! I wasn't expecting to see you till the morning!

BETH. I wasn't expecting to see you at all.

Beat.

And *cleaning.*

MARY (*apologetically*). I had to. The place is filthy. I never thought you couldn't manage.

BETH. Couldn't manage what?

MARY. You know… [the state of the place.]

BETH. No. I don't know.

MARY. Sorry. (*Pause.*) I don't mean to offend you.

BETH. You don't.

MARY. Or frighten you.

BETH (*intimidating*). You missed a bit.

MARY *turns to look behind her at the spot indicated by* BETH, *and* BETH *advances with the hammer.*

MARY. Why don't you give me that?

BETH. Where would you like it?

She closes in and MARY *squares off.*

What is it anyway? Money for drugs again? It's always that. I could crack your head open like a hairy coconut. Happy as I go. Or – (*Swinging her hammer.*) you could just get out of my house!

MARY (*dodging*). No.

BETH. Get out of my –

MARY. No!

She takes another good swing at MARY.

BETH. Get –

MARY. NO! I can't! It's too late.

BETH. Go home, you – !

MARY. I can't go home! That's the *point*!

BETH. I'm *warning* you –

> BETH *swings again and* MARY *grabs her by the wrist and relieves her of the hammer.*

MARY. No, I am warning YOU, Edith! And I am not leaving!

> BETH*'s hackles rise.*

BETH. Pardon me?

MARY. You heard me.

BETH (*indignant*). I heard Edith.

MARY. *Mrs Patten* then.

> *Beat.*

BETH. Am I supposed to *know* you?

MARY. What?

BETH. Am I supposed to know you?

> *Beat.*

MARY. Do you not… recognise me?

BETH. No.

MARY. Are you sure?

BETH. Quite.

> *Beat.*

> Apologies if I'm supposed to.

MARY. It's okay. You're not, I suppose. You're *not* supposed to.

> MARY *tucks the hammer into her belt.*

> I'll hang on to this.

BETH. Why? You'll never use it.

MARY. Don't tempt me. (*Pause. Suddenly piqued.*) No. People like you are *not* supposed to know people like me. Are you?

BETH. What are you talking about? Who are you? What do you know about people like me?

MARY. I know that people like you are...

MARY *eyeballs her.*

BETH. What? Are what?

Beat.

MARY. Rich.

BETH *laughs.*

BETH. Ha! So now *I suppose* you think you know all about me.

MARY. Enough.

BETH. You know squat. (*Pause.*) Wait a minute, how do you know my name?

MARY. I heard them talking about you in the store one time. After you went out. That you used to be married to some big-shot money-man. They said you used to be a real looker. Before that I just always thought of you as the TV-dinner lady. Which is funny. Cos you don't have a TV, do you? But you shop for TV dinners every day.

BETH. You've been *watching* me?

MARY. In your fur coat.

BETH. *Stalking* me?!

MARY. No. I used to say hello to you. Every single day for years when I worked down the avenue. American Attire Disribution Limited. You can see their water tank from that window. I thought you seemed sad and lonely and I was trying to be nice. Every day. Remember me now?

BETH (*indignant*). I am not lonely.

MARY. Yeah? All that time I never saw you *with* someone.

BETH. I have people.

MARY. They said in the store you don't have anyone.

BETH. Did they?

MARY. Husband gone, no children.

BETH. I have a child.

MARY. Oh?

BETH. Yes, 'oh'. John.

MARY. Really? John. (*Alarmed*.) Is he here? He's not here. I would have seen him. Is he here?

BETH. He's busy.

MARY. Busy away?

BETH *doesn't answer.*

Off spending his trust fund? Blondes and sports cars?

BETH. Your originality is so refreshing.

Beat.

MARY. You really don't remember me?

BETH. Believe me.

MARY. I guess no one can remember what they never really looked at. Not even down their nose. But I looked at you. Haven't for a while though. Obviously. No call to be in this neighbourhood any more. But I kept seeing you anyway. In my head. Going in and out of here. This huge brownstone. All to yourself. Got me thinking –

BETH. What? That I was vulnerable and defenceless? That you'd break in and do a little *spring-cleaning* before burglarising me?

MARY. I'm not here to burgle you.

BETH. What are you here for then?

MARY. I don't want your things.

BETH. What *do* you want?

MARY. Not your little things anyway.

BETH. What then?

MARY. Not even your money really.

BETH. What do you want?!

> MARY *squares off to her.*
>
> What?!
>
> *Beat.*
>
> WHAT?!

MARY. The house.

> *Beat.*
>
> I want your house.
>
> *Beat.*

BETH (*aghast*). You can't just come in and take a person's house!

MARY. Why not?

BETH. Because you just can't.

MARY. The bank just came in and took mine.

BETH. But there are laws. Statutes! Or they'd all be doing it.

MARY. Who would?

BETH. Poor people. Riff-raff – hoodlum types – out there.

MARY. I think you'll find they're in here now.

BETH. You might be *in*. But you're not *staying*. You look like a nice girl. A bit... tired, shall we say. Why don't you just go on home?

MARY. Because I don't have one.

BETH. Well, you're not waltzing in here and getting this one. This is my house. It's been in my husband's family for generations.

MARY. Yes. (*Tartly.*) Bit of a monopoly that, isn't it?

She lets that land and, speaking as she goes, she drags over a big holdall and dumps out a load of bedrolls on to the floor where she has swept.

Seems entirely reasonable to me that someone else should get a turn now for a while.

She lays out the first bedroll.

BETH. What are you doing?

MARY. I'm going to use this room. Till we settle in, anyway. Doesn't look like anyone else is using it, so it shouldn't be a problem.

She roots out a teddy bear and puts it on top of the roll.

BETH (*recoiling*). There are children here?

MARY. Where else would they be?

BETH. In this house? There are children in this house?

MARY (*checking out the window*). They're asleep in the car outside. But probably not for much longer.

She gets the carpet sweeper and starts sweeping a rectangle for the next roll.

I thought I'd use the time to come in ahead and check things out. Good job. I don't know how you live with these floors.

BETH. I don't look down.

MARY. Or out the windows either. Don't you have a cleaner? You could keep the whole of Puerto Rico in business, cleaning this place.

BETH. Don't think that cleaning my house is going to give you title.

MARY *stops sweeping. She flips the second bedroll onto the clean patch of carpet.*

Or that you can throw down a few scraps and stake a claim like it's the Wild West!

MARY. Why not? Why can't I?

BETH. Oh be rational.

MARY. I am being rational.

BETH. No you're not!

MARY. Yes I am.

BETH. No you're – !

MARY. Yes I – !

BETH. No – !

MARY. WHY?! Why is this not rational?! You're here all by yourself in a huge inherited mansion that you did nothing to actually earn, while me and my kids are out on the street with absolutely nothing when all I ever did was work and pay my way? (*Pause.*) So here I am and what's not rational? I mean, did you ever even make a payment on this house?

No answer.

Ever have a job?

No answer.

Did you ever do anything?

BETH. Some things of some import.

MARY. What? Match your shoes to your handbag?

BETH. I think I'd've preferred a regular burglary. Even a bit of battery.

MARY. Play your cards right.

BETH. Don't blame me. It's just the way the world works.

MARY. I know what way the world works! You get born rich, marry rich and sit on your rich ass so more rich can fall in your lap, while *I* get to slop buckets of geriatric piss and shit out of Moe's Old Folk's Home three nights a week on top of my *real* job because –

BETH. Oh, yadda yadda yadda. I am very sorry you couldn't have been born under a jollier star but none of that is my fault, and you, are not my problem.

MARY. I am now.

Beat.

BETH *turns on her heel and starts stuffing the second roll into the holdall.*

I was more than happy to earn my living – what are you doing?

BETH. Packing up your soapbox.

MARY. Don't you touch that!!!

BETH *continues packing.*

BETH. I'm bored now.

MARY. I said *don't touch it*!

MARY *grabs the holdall.*

This is the very last thing I have left after everything I worked for DON'T YOU TOUCH IT!!!

She stares hard at BETH.

I apologise if my little existence isn't quite entertaining enough for you. But I think you'll find it's all about to get a bit more interesting. Cos, see, when the Government took my job and gave it to some cheaper Malaysian, there wasn't really much I could do about that. Or when American Attire Distribution Limited found some loophole to say they didn't have to give me any severance, or my pension, not really much I could do about that either. Or when the bank took my house even though after *twelve years of payments* I'd already paid them *twice* what it's worth, somehow I still owe them twice that amount again. Go figure. The bank manager didn't even bother to put his tie on – I guess he's bored taking people's homes by now. Nothing I seemed to be able to do about any of anything except shut up, roll over and keep taking it all quietly up the ass like a good little poor person's supposed to. Because that's just the way the world works. (*Ominously.*) But *now*, Mrs Patten, now Child Protection Services are coming after my *children*. Because, surprise surprise, after everything's been taken away from me, it seems I don't have what it takes to look after them any more. Fancy that. Everything, systematically taken away from me, one by one, till I find myself standing here in the middle of the night in the middle of all your excess like a *peeled snail* with her *children under threat* and you think I'm being *irrational*?! Let me tell you, there is nothing, nothing at all, that I *won't* do now. And given the circumstances, anything that I *do* do, will be quite RATIONAL!

Beat.

BETH. Maybe you just didn't work hard enough.

MARY. Jesus Christ.

Beat.

BETH. Well, maybe you didn't.

MARY. What do you even know about hard work? Maybe you seen some on TV one time. Two hundred people got laid off! Just a couple of blocks from here. Though that might as well be galaxies to you.

BETH. They all coming to live here too?

MARY. Maybe they should!

BETH. A Communist we have. This is funny.

MARY. This is not funny! I have three little boys and two goldfish out there and nowhere to put them but the back seat of a clapped-out station wagon I can't even afford to put gas in any more! And you get all this all to yourself for no good reason! *A Manhattan brownstone!* And you don't even appreciate it. I mean, look at this crap!

She pulls out lumps of the carpet sweeper's innards from the box.

BETH. That's decades of my life you've got there. Maybe even some of the best bits.

MARY. And it stinks!

BETH. Go next door then. Take their house.

MARY. Like a urinal.

BETH. Broken drains.

MARY. You shouldn't be allowed to have it. There should be a law against you. What you're doing is criminal.

BETH. No dear. I think you'll find what you're doing is criminal. I am living my own quiet life, getting in nobody's way and asking for nothing.

MARY. You never had to ask! I thought I didn't either. I was stupid enough to think I could actually work hard, buy a little house for my kids –

MARY *strides to the window and checks below again, still speaking.*

– work harder, and send them to college! I certainly never thought I could do that the only way us 'riff-raff' types know – the 'hard work' way – and still fail my children. While yours I suppose, is just going to acquire all this cos you finally managed to do something useful with your life and *die*!

BETH (*quietly*). I want you out of this house.

MARY. I'm in it now and I'm going nowhere. Getting to this point was the hard part. Staying's going to be real easy.

BETH. You think so?

MARY. I think so.

BETH. How'd you even get in here?

MARY. Determination.

MARY *starts to lay out the bedroll again.*

Amazing what you can do when you have children.

BETH. Indeed.

MARY. Even you might do the same.

BETH. Even you might be amazed.

MARY. There is nothing I would not do for them.

BETH. Really?

MARY. Not that you'd ever have to. Do anything for your –

BETH. Go to friends. Like any normal person.

MARY *laughs*.

MARY. You think I didn't try that? Most of them are in the same situation. There is no one else and no place else. If there was, I'd be there.

BETH. What about their father?

MARY (*coldly*). Something else I couldn't give them. (*Closing the subject.*) Coming here was so... obvious. I don't know why I didn't think of it sooner. Instead of letting things get so... Anyway, why should I go to friends and stuff us all into some already-stuffed apartment with all this lying empty here?

BETH. Not quite empty. What exactly do you propose *I* do?

MARY. Well, I won't do a United Banks of America and turf you out. I'm nicer.

BETH. That *is* nice.

MARY. I don't mind sharing.

BETH. I don't do sharing.

MARY. You do what you like. You've got plenty of other options. Shack up at The Astor. See the world. I don't care. I know what I'd do if I was in your shoes.

BETH *looks down at her sandals*.

BETH. Do you indeed?

MARY. But I'm staying.

BETH. This is total lunacy.

MARY. Is it? I really don't know why more people aren't doing it.

BETH. Because they're not all total lunatics. Now, I am very sorry for all your woes, but do you think you could leave now and go have your nervous breakdown some place else?

MARY. You know something?

Beat.

You're a horrible woman.

Beat.

I thought you never said hello back to me because you were sad. A sad and lonely old lady in her crusty fur coat. But no. Just horrible.

MARY *laughs.*

And to think I used to wish I could *be* you. (*Pause.*) Well, be a woman who didn't have to wring herself out with worry every day – just be able to open my purse and solve all my problems. Money can't buy you happiness my ass. But I never actually thought I'd actually come here. Into your house. Or anything. Not until tonight. Not until I was putting my boys to bed, the last night I had a bed to put them in, not until I couldn't ignore it any longer...

Beat.

That I couldn't look after my own children.

Beat.

That I had absolutely nothing for them. My lovely, sleeping, trusting children. Can you imagine what that feels like?

Beat.

Actually, it felt like nothing. Like I knew it was too big to even try to feel. That it might kill me if I did. So I just sat there. In their bedroom. And then a lovely calmness started to come over me. Cos suddenly I knew what I was going to do. And I just started packing. Cos I knew where I was going. It was so obvious. TV-dinner lady's house.

Beat.

BETH. Well, don't bother *un*packing. This is not a shelter for the sick and indigent.

MARY. No, just a prize for the rich and greedy.

BETH. Yes. But it is my prize.

BETH *inadvertently stands on the bedroll.*

MARY. Get off there!

BETH. This is my house!

MARY. AND THAT IS MY SON'S BED YOU'RE STANDING ON! GET OFF IT!

The air is massively charged between them as the women glare at each other from either side of the bedroll.

BETH. Let me give you something.

MARY *stares at her in anticipation.*

I have diazepam.

MARY. You should take some then!

BETH *suddenly appears distracted, concerned – listening for something.*

BETH. Shush!

MARY (*apprehensive*). Wha–

BETH. Sh!

She listens some more, then tries to tiptoe vaguely in the direction of the door, still listening, staring at the ground.

(*Whispering.*) Damn shoes are so loud.

MARY. They're very big.

BETH. Room for blisters and life's other irritations.

She listens some more.

MARY. What?

BETH (*flippantly*). Rats.

Beat.

MARY (*barely disguised alarm*). There are rats here?

BETH. It's an extra feature.

BETH *decides the coast is clear and returns her attention to* MARY.

She clocks her fear.

Don't tell me you're scared?

MARY. No.

BETH. Of a little rat? How are you going to win the revolution?! (*Laughing.*) And beds on the floor. Tut tut tut.

MARY. Why don't you call in pest control?

BETH. Same reason I didn't call in the cops for you. Or the boys in the white coats. Where would be the fun? If you don't like them, don't stand there. See those holes? Bolt-holes. You're standing right in their path.

MARY *moves away 'casually' and stumbles over her son's bed.*

You'd never survive one night here.

MARY. I'm fine!

Beat.

BETH. Watch out!

MARY *jumps and squeals.*

MARY. Where?

BETH. Behind you!

MARY *is absolutely terrified but she holds her ground.*

MARY. *Where?!*

BETH. Smash it!

MARY. What?!

BETH. Smash it with your big hammer!

MARY (*revolted*). No!

BETH. Smash it!

MARY. No!

BETH. Smash it!

MARY. *No!*

BETH. You're scared of a little rat and I'm supposed to be scared of you? I'm quaking in my big shoes here.

MARY (*gritted teeth*). I'm not scared.

BETH (*rounding*). Good. Because I'm not wasting my time entertaining any yella-bellies. There's a lot you could learn from that rat. Remarkably adaptive creature. Teeth so strong it can chew through walls to get to where it needs to be. Squeeze its backbone through the smallest of holes and – (*Laden.*) pop up uninvited in my house. But even that rat understands that if it wants to *stay* here – that's going to require an even bigger deployment of teeth and backbone –

MARY *is nodding.*

– or else it's –

BETH *slaps her hands together viciously – like a large rat trap.*

I earned this house and earned it hard! Every last lump of stone in it. Abhorrent to you that I should get it 'for nothing', but here you are with your hand out and nothing to tender but a hard-luck story!

MARY. I'm not looking for something for nothing! When did I say that?! How about I clean for you?

BETH. Ha!

MARY. Plenty of work right there.

BETH. You'd have to be a lot more useful than that.

MARY. And cook! I'm sure we could think of an arrangement!

BETH. I can think of an arrangement all right.

MARY (*pleading*). Things could be a whole lot better for you too, you know. Company. Proper meals. Help if there was ever an… (*Doesn't like to say 'emergency'*.) It could even be… *nice*.

BETH. *Nice?*

MARY. Why not? It could. I could paint. It could be lovely here. Window boxes.

BETH *laughs*.

Why not? Why not? It could be so *easy*! It could be *nice*!

BETH. Some things just aren't nice! You should know that.

MARY. But we could make them –

BETH. Not this.

MARY. Why not? *Why not?!*

BETH *stops laughing*.

BETH. Because the Manhattan Pattens don't do philanthropy.

Beat.

MARY. So I heard. Too busy taking care of *themselves*. Not interested in making the world a nicer place for anyone but themselves – (*Looking around her.*) and couldn't even succeed in that!

BETH. Interesting new tactic.

MARY. The man in the store said your husband was a grade-A bastard in his day.

BETH. The man in the store was not misinformed.

MARY. Quite the ladies' man.

BETH. But then I did find his depravity easier when directed at other women.

MARY. They do say if you marry a rich man you have to work hard for your money.

BETH. They would be quite right.

MARY. Not too bothered then when he croaked it? Couldn't find it in your heart? And your son obviously hoofed it out of here fast enough too. Are you just so horrible everyone has to get away from you?

BETH. I wish it would work on you.

MARY. You're going to end up a few newspaper inches – 'Unidentified Corpse Found in Brownstone.' (*Adding.*) 'Devoured by Rats.'

BETH. Keep this up and they might be eating you first.

MARY. Everything you have to give him and where is he?

BETH. Who?

MARY *is starting to lose control.*

MARY. Your son. Disowned, is he? Something scandalous, is it? Black sheep? He's not here anyway. Looking after you. *Earning* his big house. Letting you live like this –

BETH (*very calmly*). Stop.

MARY. – like a derelict! My boys would never do that to me! Off waiting in the wings somewhere –

BETH *walks to within a foot of* MARY.

BETH. Stop.

MARY. – wishing you would hurry up and kick the bucket –

BETH *puts her arm out and holds* MARY *by the elbows.*

– so he can come back here and get his lily-white paws on MY HOUSE!

BETH. I said stop.

Beat.

MARY *has stopped. She starts to come to and is genuinely shocked at herself.*

MARY. Oh my God, I'm so sorry, Edith. I'm so sorry. I didn't mean to upset you –

BETH. Of course you did. Of course you meant to upset me. That's the sole reason you're here. To upset me. Even in your lopsided brain you didn't think I was actually going to *give* you my house. You just wanted to rid yourself on me. You let your own life go to hell so you thought you'd come in here and heave up all your righteous indignation – make yourself feel like your hardship gives you more worth than my privilege! That your failure makes you a better person than my – …! I earned every single thing I got here. In ways that give me value far beyond my husband's money. In ways far beyond your tiny comprehension!

Suddenly a male voice bellows from offstage.

HAL. WOMAN!

MARY *jumps and looks terrified.*

BETH *doesn't flinch.*

BETH. Even if I didn't deserve the half of it. But here you are thinking you deserve to take it all away from me.

HAL. WOMAN!!!

BETH. And if I was really cruel? (*Pause.*) I'd give it to you.

BETH *suddenly flips the bedroll toward the back wall.*

MARY *is flapping about in a panic.*

MARY. Who is – ?!

BETH. Backbone. Teeth.

MARY. What?

BETH. You're going to need them now.

BETH *steels herself.*

The door opens and HAL *enters.*

He is very dishevelled, wearing pyjamas, and using a stick. He has the tell-tale chorea and muscle-wastage of Leon Scallick's Disease, and although physically frail, he is very, very forceful. His speech is only disturbed in that he often gets to the end of a sentence and suddenly can't remember the word he wants. He doesn't slur.

MARY, *upstage of* HAL *and unseen by him, is first stunned by his existence, then horrified by his demeanour.*

He passes close by her, moving very slowly and unsteadily, and it is clear that he stinks.

HAL *points his stick ferociously across the stage at* BETH's *feet.*

HAL. I knew it! I knew it, you dried-up old cock – ...

BETH. Sucker.

HAL. Shriveller. Get your cloven hooves out of my – ...

BETH. Shoes.

HAL. No!

BETH. Slippers.

HAL. SANDALS! You – ... you – ... you – ...

BETH. Not the C-word, Hal. You know I don't like saying that one.

HAL. Yes, that one! You're a – ... (*And the word is lost again. Annoyed.*) Give me my sandals!

BETH *slips out of the shoes and steps away.*

HAL *starts making his way across the stage towards them.*

BETH. Why don't I fetch you your slippers, Hal? They're warmer.

HAL *stops.*

HAL (*suspiciously*). Why are you being so nice?

> HAL *continues on his long journey.*

> Beside my door. I leave them beside my door. In case I need to go somewhere.

BETH. You never go anywhere.

HAL. Neither do you. But still you need to steal my sandals?

BETH. I could go somewhere.

HAL. Balls, she thinks she has. And no spunk to fill 'em. A hundred years I listen to that crap. There's the – …

BETH. Door.

> BETH *smells him now.*

> Did you do a little mistake, Hal?

HAL. Yes. I married you.

BETH. Why don't you give me your soiled –

HAL. I wouldn't give you a dry hump.

> BETH *turns deliberately to* MARY.

BETH. And to think that only *some* of that is sickness.

> HAL *turns now and sees* MARY *for the first time.*

> *She recoils under his long, hard stare.*

> HAL *turns back to* BETH *and talks about* MARY *without looking at her.*

HAL. Who's that?

BETH. A guest.

HAL. You don't have guests.

BETH. Well, I have one now.

HAL. What does she want?

BETH. Nothing much.

HAL. Get rid of her.

BETH. She wants to stay.

HAL. GET RID OF HER!

BETH *turns to* MARY.

BETH. You want to stay, don't you?

MARY *doesn't know what to do, doesn't move.*

HAL *turns to* MARY

HAL (*an imperial command*). No one looks at me.

MARY *averts her gaze.*

HAL, *shoes on now, heads for the door.*

They wait. After he's passed, MARY *lifts her head to look. It is torturous watching him.*

(*Without looking at her.*) No one looks at me!

MARY *immediately averts her gaze again.*

And fuck off with your sympathy.

(*Passing* BETH.) Get rid of her.

He slams the door.

The air settles.

Beat.

MARY (*stunned*). I thought he was dead.

HAL (*off*). I'm too mean to die!

MARY *has to sit down.*

Beat.

MARY. Does he always talk to you like that?

BETH. In sonnets and serenades?

Beat.

MARY. I thought he was dead.

BETH. You thought a lot.

MARY. I never saw him. I thought he –

BETH. He couldn't stop the disease, but he could stop people
see him 'dribble himself away out of every orifice'. So he
holed himself up in here for the past fifteen years. (*Pause*.)
And me along with him.

MARY. I'm so sorry, Edith.

Beat.

BETH. Beth.

MARY. What?

BETH. I go by the Elizabeth. Edith Elizabeth. The man in the
store not tell you that?

Beat.

'Elizabeth – Thy God is bountiful. Thy God is Abundance.
Thou shalt not want.' Ha. What's your name?

MARY. Mary.

Beat.

BETH. No room at the inn then?

The joke draws a small, ice-breaking laugh.

MARY. Don't you have help? A nurse?

BETH. I have had a succession of nurses. A parade of New
York's finest. None of them lasted more than a few weeks,
not for any amount of money, not if Hal didn't want them
here and made it hell. He wanted it that only I was privy to
his 'indignities'. (*Pause*.) That I perform 'my wifely duties'.

MARY *is shocked by the awfulness of it.*

(*Barbed*.) He had bought and paid for them after all.

Beat.

Not that that was necessary. Who could leave a sick husband?

Beat.

Till death do us part.

BETH *suddenly looks really tired.*

I just never thought it would take this long.

She sits down.

I know how awful that sounds.

MARY. No. (*Appalled.*) Fifteen years like this.

BETH. And according to his physician, there could be another fifteen in him.

MARY. Oh my –

BETH. A genetic mutation on gene IT-16 located on the long arm of chromosome 5. Leon Scallick's Disease. Something like that ever blight your little horizon? You know nothing at all about life's bitter reaches.

HAL *calls from offstage and can be heard making his way towards them again.*

HAL. YOU!

MARY *jumps up.*

HAL *enters.*

He points at BETH.

You!

BETH. Beth.

HAL. I know your name. I just don't want to say it.

She sees that his feet are bare.

BETH. Where are your shoes, Hal?

HAL. My piss-bag needs to be – ...

BETH. Emptied.

HAL. You think all of a sudden I can do that by – ...?

BETH. No.

HAL. Why are you sitting?

BETH. I'm tired.

HAL. All the cleaning?

BETH. All the dancing. All the carousing.

> HAL *suddenly spies* MARY.

All the living.

HAL. I told you to get rid of her. You want me to do it?

BETH. You might not find it so easy to get rid of this one.

HAL. This one what?

> BETH *turns to* MARY *and contemplates her hard.*

BETH. This...

HAL. What?

BETH. This. Nurse.

MARY (*simultaneous*). What?!

HAL (*simultaneous*). What?

> HAL's *left arm is seized by a furious choreaic tic.* MARY
> *stares at him, utterly repulsed.*

BETH. Nurse! Nurse!

HAL. Over my dead – ...!

BETH. No one is going to let you die, Hal.

HAL. You'll see to that, I'm sure!

BETH. Of course I'll see to that. She has years of experience.

MARY. No I don't.

BETH. You worked in an old folk's home, didn't you?

MARY. *Cleaning* it! I don't know *anything* about looking after… (*Looks at* HAL *in spasm and doesn't know what to call him*.) an old folk.

BETH. It's not that complicated –

HAL. It is if I make it!

BETH. – and I'll show you the ropes.

HAL. And I'll hang her on them!

BETH. I know he's not the prettiest of propositions. But he lives here. And if you want to live here too, help with him is what I need.

HAL. What are you talking about?!

BETH. Help, Hal, I need help! You know I do. I am not getting any younger!

HAL. Just stupider.

HAL *advances on* MARY, *demanding to be obeyed, using his stick*.

You! Get out of my – …! This is *my* – … and I want you out of it!

MARY, *albeit scared, holds her ground*.

In frustration, HAL *turns on his wife, pushing his stick against her chest*.

(*Eerily calm*.) Only you – …

BETH. Beth.

HAL. Beth. Only you.

BETH *sidesteps out from under the stick, causing* HAL *to lose his balance and stumble. His energy is draining rapidly*.

HAL. We aren't through yet. You and I. We aren't through.

BETH *takes a necklace off from around her neck – a chain with a key on it*.

BETH (*to* MARY). He needs a shot.

HAL. I don't want a – …!

He tries to thump his stick down but only drops it. He can't keep his balance without it.

BETH. Take him. I'll be one second.

MARY hesitates.

Take him!

Beat.

Take. Him.

Beat.

As HAL *teeters on the brink of falling,* MARY *grabs him.*

Good.

She turns to leave the room.

A wise decision.

MARY. What?

BETH exits.

Not knowing what else to do, MARY *just stands there holding* HAL's *limp body.*

A leer creeps over HAL's *face. A hand finds its way to* MARY's *bottom and he helps himself generously.* MARY *can't extricate herself. He is still in danger of falling if she does.*

HAL. It's in the job description. If you're thinking of staying. 'Small services.'

MARY tries to get away again.

HAL tightens his grip.

I'm allowed to handle the goods if I'm buying.

BETH re-enters with a syringe.

(*To* BETH.) You couldn't have found me one with a bit more meat on it? It's bad enough I have to look at you all day with your titties like socks full of – …

BETH. Marbles. Leave her alone, Hal.

HAL. She might as well get used to it.

BETH. He's only trying to frighten you. Believe me, he is no longer any threat in that department.

HAL. Not while there's been nothing with a heartbeat in the house.

He grins at MARY, *jerks*.

But here's a kitty-cat could stand me to attention. If she put a little effort in. If she wants to stay and play.

HAL *goes for* MARY*'s breasts.* MARY *pushes him off and* HAL *stumbles and falls to his knees.*

MARY. I'm sorry! Oh! (*To* BETH.) I'm sorry.

HAL. Kitty *likes* to play, huh?

Still in spasm, HAL *goes for his stick and starts to draw himself back up to standing.*

BETH *squirts liquid out of the syringe and holds it out to* MARY.

BETH. You do it. You might as well get started.

MARY *hesitates*.

There's not much to it.

MARY *still doesn't take it*.

You want this job or not?

Beat.

MARY *takes the syringe*.

Good. Now. Go for the hindquarters. And go in nice and steady. That way it won't hurt.

MARY *nods again, willing herself.*

Just don't hit his diaper.

A look of panic on MARY*'s face and* HAL, *now in full spasm, begins to circle her like a grotesque fighter in the ring.*

HAL. Come on then. Let's see what you got. Do your worst! I used to be a – …

BETH (*rolling her eyes*). Wrestler.

HAL. Twice Borough – …

BETH. Champion.

HAL. Yeah. You hear that? Tell her what they called me.

BETH. The Wall Street Behemoth.

HAL. Think you can take The Behemoth? Huh? Huh?

MARY *is not sure that she actually can.*

BETH. Show him who's boss this once and you'll never have to show him again.

MARY *nods and steps gingerly forward.*

You can handle him.

HAL. LIKE THIS?!

HAL *suddenly rears to his full formidable power and* MARY *jumps back in shock.*

THINK YOU CAN HANDLE ME IF *I AM LIKE THIS*?!!! IF YOU CAN'T GET *THAT* INTO ME HOW YOU GONNA GET A TUBE UP MY DICK OR AN ENEMA UP MY ASS IF *I AM LIKE THIS*!!! SOMETIMES SHE GETS ME SO SHE CAN DO BOTH AT THE SAME TIME! LIKE A *SPIT-ROAST!* THINK *YOU* CAN DO –

MARY *suddenly runs and throws herself at* HAL, *topples him, gets him straight down on the floor on his stomach and rams the needle into his behind.*

Just as quickly she jumps up and away and surveys her deed, deeply disturbed.

Even BETH *is shocked.*

MARY. Jesus Christ.

HAL, *limp, is moaning quietly.*

Beat.

(*Looking at the now empty syringe in her hand.*) What is it?

BETH. Anti-spasmodic. And something else to calm him. He'll be groggy for a while first, then calm, and then he should sleep. Merciful stuff.

HAL *moans.*

MARY. Did I hurt him?

BETH. That's the shock of losing, I'd say. No. You did well. Now he knows he can't take you on. Which is good. Because now it means you can afford to show him... compassion.

MARY *nods, uncertain.*

The diapers are all in this landing's main bathroom. Next to his bedroom. He never leaves this floor. He can't do stairs and you need to him keep off them. He took a bad fall a few months back. That smells like a runny one – you should probably get to it quick. Especially while he's like this. He has a catheter in so you don't have to worry too much about his front end –

HAL (*mournfully and druggy*). Like a stallion I used to have a stream.

BETH. – wash that with soap and water only. You don't want his member to get an infection. If it does, pour on some antiseptic and run like Lot.

MARY. Oh my –

HAL (*druggy*). Nobody's asking you to suck it.

BETH. You have to get his bile up too.

HAL (*druggy*). Generally my wife is a great help with that.

BETH. And there's ointment for his gums. I hope you've had a tetanus.

MARY *nods confusedly – yes – no – yes.*

His food has to be puréed. Or he can't swallow. Those TV dinners work best for that. He's also best fed when he's a bit sedated. The medicines are all under lock and key upstairs. Make sure they stay that way. He thinks he can do it himself but… (*Shakes her head.*) he gets confused. Be especially vigilant after he's had a shot. That's when he really gets delusions of competence. But don't worry, I'll talk you through it all again before I leave.

MARY. What?

BETH. I'll write it all down for you.

MARY. You're *leaving*?

This starts to bring HAL *to.*

HAL. No – no –

BETH. Yes, Hal.

MARY (*in total disbelief*). You can't just –

BETH. Mary will take good care of you. I know she will.

MARY (*simultaneous*). Beth –

HAL (*simultaneous*). No!

BETH. I wouldn't go if I wasn't sure of that.

HAL. You *can't*, Beth –

BETH. You don't need me. You don't want *me*. You just want a –

HAL. I want *you*!

The effort floors him again.

MARY. Beth –

BETH. *What?!* This is the only way things are going to work for you too, you know!

MARY. But you can't just walk out!

BETH. Why not? You just walked in.

MARY. But you can't just *give* me your *husband*!

BETH (*shrugging*). He comes with the house.

The women glare at each other.

What? You want my privilege but not the price I paid for it?

HAL's *stick is just beyond arm's reach and he lets out a furious moan. The women wait it out to see who'll aid him first.*

MARY *can't stand it. Disgusted at* BETH, *she goes and retrieves it for him.*

And she helps him up.

HAL *and* MARY *stand together looking at* BETH.

I apologise. I know this is a terrible thing to do... I'm just so tired... and scared. That I can't do it properly any more, Hal. That it's going to kill both of us. (*Pause.*) This is better. (*Fixing on* MARY.) You treat him well, and you'll get those next fifteen years out of him. Long enough to raise your children here. And that is my insurance. That is how I *know* you'll take good care of him. That is how I'm able to go.

Beat.

MARY. I don't know how you're able to do this.

Beat.

BETH. Sure you do. (*Pause.*) A 'lovely calmness' just came over me.

MARY. Is this a joke?

BETH. I never joke.

BETH *starts to head for the door.*

Three little boys, Hal. You'll enjoy that.

A quick tic shudders through HAL.

MARY (*a note of panic*). Are you going to go right now?

BETH. Of course not. I'll be back down first. I'll take you through it all again.

MARY. Are you going to be close by?

BETH *turns and continues towards the door.*

MARY *is left there holding* HAL, *watching her walk away.*

She suddenly calls out after her.

Beth! Wait! This is – ! I'm not sure if I – I don't – know –

BETH. What's the matter?

BETH *turns slowly.*

Got a silver spoon stuck in your gullet?

MARY *is rendered speechless.*

BETH *turns again and is gone from the room, leaving a stunned silence in her wake.*

After a moment, MARY *looks urgently towards the window and tries to get to it, but can't with* HAL *in her dependency.*

She takes him to the swivel chair behind the big desk and settles him where he slumps.

She hurries to the window and pulls the curtain aside to try and get a good view of the car and check on her children. Nothing she sees seems to alert her to the children being awake.

BETH *can be heard moving about above them.*

MARY *hangs on to the curtains and gives in to a crying that has been building up for weeks.*

HAL, *as if drawn into some sort of reverie by the desk, lays his hands on it.*

Beat.

HAL (*quietly*). Why are we in this room?

MARY *turns, her crying punctured.*

MARY. It was the cleanest.

Beat.

HAL. We never come in this room.

Beat.

MARY. Probably why it's the cleanest.

She watches him stroking the desk.

HAL. This is my room.

MARY *suddenly goes for the window-sash.*

MARY. We need some air in here.

Despite her best attempt, she can't get it open.

(*Making the discovery.*) They're *nailed*!

Why are they nailed?

HAL. So I don't jump.

MARY. Do you want to?

HAL *shrugs. Maybe. Maybe not.*

(*Quietly.*) Jesus.

HAL. Get this stuff off of here.

MARY *doesn't know what he is talking about.*

HAL *bangs his fist down on the table.*

Get this stuff off of here!

MARY *jumps. She goes to and starts to clear the desk.*

HAL *doesn't take his eyes off it – watching as the leather top emerges.*

MARY *goes to strike an old desk lamp – the last thing on it.*

Leave that.

MARY *obeys and sets the lamp back down again.*

HAL leans his arms out wide across the breadth of the desk and explores the old familiar surroundings with an 'it's good to be back home' attitude.

As if he is drawing up power from the very desk itself, he pulls himself up to his full height – reinstated and reinvigorated – and finally he lifts his head with perfect control.

Beat.

He tilts back in the swivel chair, lustily stroking the arms, and surveys his kingdom. A wide grin splits open his face. The charming old bastard he used to be.

Back in the saddle.

Beat.

Back in business.

He motions to MARY.

Pull up a pew.

She looks around her and goes for the nearest thing to hand, pulling an old wobbly chair off a heap behind her. She seats herself across the desk from HAL. Her chair is that bit too low.

HAL drinks her in.

MARY (*nervous*). It's a bit like being at the bank.

HAL. It's exactly like being at the bank.

He flicks on the desk lamp and its glare catches her right in the eyes.

Next he opens the top drawer of the desk and lifts out a small wooden box which he places on top. He lifts the lid and breathes the smell in deep. Out of the box he takes a fat cigar and rolls it lovingly around his fingers.

Got matches?

MARY *shakes her head apologetically.*

Me either. Not allowed to play with them.

He bites off the top of the cigar. He leans back in the chair, inhales vigorously and blows the 'smoke' out, even going for a few smoke rings. Tipping his 'ash', he leaves the cigar to rest on top of the box.

That done, he goes for a bottom drawer and lifts out a very expensive-looking bottle of single malt, along with a tumbler, and puts it up on the desk.

He pours, and holds the drink out to MARY.

MARY. I don't drink.

HAL. Today you do.

MARY stands to reach and takes a small draught. HAL manages to stand and leans in close to MARY and takes the drink vicariously through her. She goes 'caaa' and he lets the drink shudder through him.

He pours again.

Another.

MARY obeys. This time she gulps down the full hefty measure.

HAL *waits for the 'caaa'.*

Feel it going down?

She nods.

Get the click in your chest?

She nods.

He nods.

Good. Cos you just might need it.

She sets the glass down.

Just might need some bottle.

He motions for MARY *to sit again. She does.*

He suddenly cracks his knuckles and swings into jolly business.

You got one hell of an offer from the pterodactyl!

MARY *is not sure how to respond.*

She played a beauty. If one of my executive boys put together a deal like that, he'd find himself with a coupla extra zeros and a shiny new car at the end of the month. A beauty. (*Summarising.*) So. You, accompanied by three little boys, get to live in this house, for as long as you can keep this old bastard this side of the grave?

MARY. I wouldn't put it that way.

HAL. What way would you put it?

She can't answer.

Even got you to prove you're up to the job. You work out? Learn yourself some of that Chink stuff? Bet she couldn't believe her luck when you washed up.

MARY. I really will take good care of you.

HAL. Mm-hmm.

MARY. I think it could work.

HAL. Oh, yes. I think it could work *very* well. I think you and I could see eye to eye. I like a girl with...

He deliberately pauses – MARY *is not sure if she is supposed to come up with the word or not.*

Balls.

(*Smiling.*) Not very *nice*, though, is it? Not very nice for your children, is it? With old Harold here. Promising to be on his very best *not*-nice behaviour. For which I am held in international esteem and mightily revered.

A short leery spasm of the head.

You don't stand a dick's hope in a convent here. Apologies if that somewhat pisses on your...

He couldn't be bothered to finish the sentence.

MARY. Bubble?

HAL. *Bubble?!* I'll piss on your bubble! It's a PARADE! You piss on a – ...!

MARY. So I'll keep them away from you! Look. I am not exactly crazy about any of this either, but this is the first lifeline anyone has thrown me in a very long time and right now it is my only option!

HAL. Is it indeed?

MARY. Yes! And so, crazy as it is –

HAL starts to shake his head slowly.

– I am doing what I have to and I am taking it! And you might as well get – !

HAL. Poor Beth. Poor poor Nurse Betsy. (*Pause.*) Lay it on thick, did she?

HAL suddenly bangs his fist down on the desk.

She played you for a sucker is what she did! Stitched you right up! But don't worry. I'll unstitch you. Because she is not getting out of this house. Not while I am still in it!

He stops and controls himself – leans in across the desk.

(*Conspiratorially.*) Do you want to know why she really stays with me? Till the bitter end? My devoted wife?

Beat.

So she can make damn sure it *is* bitter.

MARY shakes her head.

Oh, yes. And long. Long and bitter.

MARY. No. That's –

HAL. And want to know why *you're* here? (*Admiring* BETH*'s brilliance*.) Because tonight she saw a way to make sure it's long and bitter without her having to stick around to do it herself. Cos she has you all stitched up to do it for her. To keep me truckin' till Judgement Day, cos you and three little boys are screwed if you don't. Oh, she played a beauty. I could almost love her. (*Pause.*) Too bad she forgot who she was playing with.

MARY *shakes her head – not believing a word of it.*

MARY. No –

HAL. Yes. Did you think you were here to nurse?

MARY *nods tentatively.*

To dispense care and 'compassion'? Not currencies we trade in round here. Gotta read the small print, rookie. The real job description. The real reason you're here.

MARY. No. No. There's no way someone would do that.

HAL. You don't know shit about what someone would do!

This halts MARY *– she knows a little of it.*

MARY. But why? Why would she…?

HAL. To punish me.

MARY. For what?

Half a beat.

HAL. There has to be a reason?

Beat.

(*Shrugging.*) Maybe there used to be a reason, who knows. But it's of little consequence now. Things just are what they are now. Don't try and fathom the black hole of my wife's mind. Just believe me when I tell you it's what she's doing. And ask yourself, are you prepared to do it for her? Are you able? That woman up there has deep reserves of spite and vengeance to draw on. Like a wounded Apache squaw. What have you got? Because, believe me, she is not 'giving me away'. She is attempting to exact a *very* high price. That, I am telling you, you cannot pay.

MARY (*tentatively*). Are you telling me she's – … she's – …

HAL (*'helping' her*). Keeping me alive against my will?

Beat.

MARY *nods.*

HAL *bursts out laughing.*

Why on earth would *I* not want to be alive?! Look at me! I'm *bursting* with life!

He lets the smile slide off his face and leans in.

I *live* for that woman. This might be hell but there's still a little bit of heaven here for as long as I am watching her in hell with me. And that is why she's not getting out of here.

MARY. I don't understand.

HAL. You don't have to. You just have to leave.

MARY. You're just saying all this to make me want to go!

HAL. Oh, no. (*All smiles.*) I am going to provide a much better incentive to make you want to go.

MARY (*nervously*). What?

HAL *starts rummaging through the desk drawers looking for something.*

HAL (*happy as he goes*). See, I like things just the way they are. With me and Betsy. Betsy and me. She wants to punish me? Fine. I'll take it. Aha!

He has found something.

But she sticks around to dole it out. Because that is *her* punishment.

MARY. What?

HAL *puts a very business-looking folder up on the desk.*

HAL. What's your name?

MARY. Pardon me?

HAL. What's your name?

MARY. Mary. What's that?

HAL. Mary what?

MARY. Davies.

HAL. Got a pen, Mary Davies?

MARY. No.

HAL. Check your purse.

MARY. I don't have a pen.

HAL. Check.

> *She gets up to check.*
>
> MARY *rummages in her bag, and does indeed find a pen.*
>
> *She hands it to* HAL.
>
> *He takes it off her, looks at it, studies it, and clicks it a few times.*
>
> Thank you – (*Writing her name with a big flourish.*) Mary Davies.

MARY. You think you can just write a cheque and I'll just go away?

HAL. Why not?

MARY. How do I even know it's real?

HAL. What, you think I keep a stash of dummies back here? (*Sardonically.*) In case of an event *just like this*? Course it's real! You get a cheque with my name on it, lady, and you're laughing all the way to the Treasury. Wouldn't you say?

MARY. I guess so.

HAL. Excellent! Throw enough cash around and you can fix anything.

> *Knocking victoriously on the desk.*
>
> Many's a fine deal was clinched across this desk. This was my father's desk. And his. And his. Chasing the green is what flows through all of us. Like a gene.

Stroking the desk lovingly.

But I surpassed them all. Nobody did deals like I did deals.

Unable to help himself.

I sold things that didn't exist, to fools with no money to buy 'em, who borrowed from banks with no bullion to back them up, and I took all that nothing, and I turned it into personal millions. Oh, yes, many's a fine shenanigans across this desk. (*Pen to cheque.*) Now –

MARY. People like you are the reason I lost my job and my home.

HAL (*busy, casual*). No. People like *you* are the reason you lost your job and your home.

MARY. What?

HAL. I'm only saying, don't blame the winners for being a loser. Bad sportsmanship.

MARY. *Sportsmanship?* The only sport you ever played was how to fuck people over for every cent you could get!

HAL. And all I want to do now is give you some of it back.

MARY. I'm not sure if I want it. God knows how many thousands of lives you completely destroyed just to get it!

HAL. I find your price and you won't be worrying about that.

MARY. We're not all like you, you know! What makes you think I even have a price?

HAL. Because everyone does. It's an immutable truth.

MARY. Really? Maybe I'd prefer to stick an enema up your ass!

HAL *laughs*.

Yeah. Maybe I'd prefer to stick around and take *that* option. It would be more honest. And I'm pretty sure I could even get to *enjoy* the job!

Beat.

HAL (*pondering the word*). Honest.

He has a small tic.

MARY. Never hear that word before?

HAL. No no, I heard it before. (*Pause.*) Out of the mouths of paupers.

MARY. You are *so* – ...!

HAL. Yeah yeah yeah, I tell you what – you take a few minutes and you grandstand all you like if it makes you feel better – but I am telling you – you are going to take this money. Know how I know?

MARY. No.

HAL. Cos I know something about you.

He clicks the pen a few times.

About all of human nature.

MARY. What?

HAL (*laying it out*). The only reason you, and people like you, are *honest*, is because you have never had the opportunity to be anything else. Other than that, it's in you, exactly the same as it's in me, to *not* be. Pay taxes?

MARY. What?

HAL. Do you pay taxes?

MARY. Of course I do.

HAL. How?

MARY. At source.

HAL. Mm-hmm. No chance of a fiddle there then. Ever had an expense account?

MARY. No.

HAL. Access to the books? Cash?

MARY. No.

HAL. Clock in or write your own time sheet?

MARY. Clock in.

HAL. Ever take the stationery home?

MARY. No.

HAL (*without looking*). This here pen has American Attire
Distribution Limited on it.

Checkmate.

HAL *clicks the pen a couple more times without taking his
eyes off* MARY.

MARY *shrinks.*

MARY. It's just a pen.

HAL. It's just a lousy pen, but it was all you could get and you
took it. I might have a bigger stationery store to pilfer but the
inclination's exactly the same. You cream what you are *able.*
So stop pissing about, cream this and get out of my house!

He scribbles on the cheque and pushes it over to MARY.

She refuses to look at it.

Look at it!

MARY *remains steadfast.*

Look at it. You might as well see what you're turning down.
The cost of piety. It'll make a great story to tell your boys
some day. I'm sure they'll be really proud of you. From
whatever dead-end job or prison cell they end up in.

MARY *bristles.*

There's plenty enough there to buy three boys a very
different future. You want a white picket fence and a Lassie
dog and an Oldsmobile? You can't get that shit on a worker's
salary any more. Anybody getting that now, is finding
another way to get it. Forget honest.

Beat.

Look.

Beat.

MARY *glances down but gives nothing away.*

You liked that, didn't you?

MARY. I don't like any of this.

HAL *pulls the cheque back to himself and, with sweeping largesse, adds what could only be a couple more zeros.*

HAL. Like it better now?

MARY *looks at the cheque. This time her eyes remain on it.*

And I can even throw in the two most celebrated words in the English language. (*Rolling them around on his tongue.*) Tax-free.

Beat.

Go on. Pick it up. Feel it. It's nice. Money is nice. Money just wants to give you things.

A door closes upstairs and BETH *can be heard can the landing.*

What the fuck is the matter with you? Can you not read?!

BETH *can be heard coming down the stairs.*

You're going to turn down an opportunity like this? For *what*?!

BETH *can be heard heaving bags along the hallway outside the room.*

Welfare cheques?!

MARY. Double it.

HAL (*straight in*). Done.

MARY *can't help but jolt a little.*

(*Amending and initialling.*) Yip. Shoulda gone for triple. Too late now. Never mind.

He finishes filling in the cheque and hands it to MARY.

As she reaches for it he takes it away again. MARY *is left with her hand out and empty as* HAL *holds the cheque aloft.*

You are mine now, Mary Davies. And you keep your mouth shut unless I tell you to open it and tell you what to say.

He presents the cheque.

MARY *hesitates in taking it.*

The door starts to open and she grabs it quick and pockets it.

HAL *throws the chequebook back into a drawer –*

(*Politely.*) May I keep the pen?

– and he throws the pen in after the chequebook.

You've probably got stacks of them anyway.

And enter BETH.

Almost like an allergic reaction to the sight of her, HAL *has to bring a few strong jerks under control.*

An expensive-looking relic of another era, BETH *is clad in a '90s Chanel-type suit which doesn't quite fit her any more. She has made an attempt at her hair and lipstick, her fur coat is over one arm, and her shoes do, in fact, match her handbag.*

Well well well.

He wheels his swivel chair out from behind the desk to get the full view.

If it isn't – … (*Struggles but gets it.*) Nancy Reagan. Come to walk amongst us.

She puts her bag and coat down on a chair.

Give us a twirl.

She just ignores him.

Like the lipstick. You look like you've just had a good suck off somebody's jugular. Suits you.

BETH. I thought you'd have been asleep by now, Hal.

HAL. Nope. Wide awake.

BETH. Would you like me to give you another shot?

HAL. Nope.

BETH. Aren't you feeling tired? You should be –

HAL. No, Beth. Positively *pert*.

Beat.

BETH *turns to* MARY.

BETH (*smiling*). Acquaintances are going well then?

HAL. It's nice to have something to look at that isn't fossilised.

BETH (*staying on* MARY). Good. That's good. (*Pause.*) The sun will be beating down hard soon.

BETH *goes to the curtain, lifts it and looks down.*

On your car. Where you've parked it. It's going to be hot today.

She turns around again.

You can put your boys in John's room. It's big. And it still has boy's things. And – well, I – it's clean. I keep that one…

HAL. Why? In case he comes home?

She ignores him.

BETH. I'll help you bring them up if you like?

MARY *looks to* HAL *for a cue – seems he is playing a long game.*

Don't worry about him. He can't get up there. (*Gently urging her.*) They're going to wake soon.

She takes the chain and key off from around her neck and moves to MARY, *taking her two hands in hers.*

She speaks with complicity, trying to keep HAL *out of it, trying not to get upset.*

This is the key to the medicine cabinet. Upstairs in my room. I've written it all out for you. Everything you need to know. I'll take you up and show you if you like?

MARY *shakes her head.*

Okay. It's all very clear.

Beat.

Thank you.

HAL *is enjoying the show.*

BETH *lets go of* MARY*'s hands.* MARY *opens them and stares down at the bunch of keys deposited there.* BETH *turns towards* HAL.

Released, MARY *immediately goes to check on her children.*

I'm sorry, Hal.

HAL. You will be.

BETH. I'm… I just can't… (*Pause.*) She'll take good care of you.

Beat.

Hal?

No response.

She turns to go.

HAL. No goodbye kiss?

BETH *goes to* HAL. *She leans down to kiss him on the cheek but* HAL *turns his head and gets her full on the mouth. Some of her lipstick rubs off.*

Aw, shucks. That made me feel all warm and runny inside. Give that woman a gong. Off you pop then –

BETH. Beth.

HAL. Mm-hmm. Off you pop, nursey.

BETH *makes for her bag and coat.*

Not you, nursey. My other nursey.

BETH. Sorry?

HAL. Mary Davies, nursey. Mary Davies here was just leaving. Weren't you, Mary Davies?

BETH *turns to look at* MARY – *caught now under the glare of both expectant stares*.

Show her.

MARY *is frozen*.

Show her.

Reluctantly MARY *takes the cheque from her pocket and holds it out to* BETH.

BETH *walks towards the cheque, takes it and reads it*.

BETH. What's this?

HAL. Her severance pay. I'm generous. But you are worth it, my little carcinoma. So. Everybody happy. Money does that. (*To* MARY.) Get your stuff.

MARY (*to* BETH). I'm sorry, Be–

HAL. Take your kickback and scram!

She hesitates.

MARY. Can I have it? (*The cheque*.)

Beat.

BETH. This? (*Handing it over*.) Oh, yes. Of course you can. That bank closed its doors years ago.

MARY. What?

BETH. That bank is bust.

HAL (*most indignant*). No it's not!

BETH. Please, Hal, you were largely responsible for closing it. (*To* MARY.) I expected better from you – nothing less from him – but better from you, you stupid girl. Your little cheque here is nothing more than a museum piece. Something – (*Turning to* HAL.) its drawer was quite aware of when he wrote it.

HAL*'s left side is gripped in a quick sudden spasm.*

HAL. I was n– …!

BETH. Stop lying. You're rusty.

HAL. THAT CHEQUE IS – …!

BETH. Fine. (*To* MARY.) Take it then. Take the cheque and leave here and bring it to the bank and see how you get on. Go.

MARY *can't move.*

HAL. Go on. Go!

She still can't move.

Fine. (*Pulling open the drawers.*) If it makes everybody happy I'll draw from a different bank. Jesus, I'll write ten cheques.

BETH (*to* MARY). And put a stop on all of them as soon as you are out the door.

HAL. Why would I do that? It's not like I have much use for the money any more.

BETH. It's not like *that* would stop you.

HAL. She can trust me.

BETH. Do you think she's *that* stupid?

HAL. What choice does she have?

BETH (*to* MARY). *Are* you that stupid?!

MARY *can't answer.*

Look at him.

MARY *looks at* HAL, *smiling, trying his best to look trustworthy.*

Are you that stupid?

HAL*'s head is suddenly gripped by another tic.*

MARY. No.

BETH *smiles.*

BETH. Good.

HAL (*to* BETH, *seething*). You're a – ...! You think that's the only bank account I can stop up? Think I can't stop yours?

BETH. Think I haven't thought of that?

HAL. You can't suck an empty – ...

BETH. Tit. I am taking only what is mine.

HAL. *Yours?* You walked in here with a pittance of a dowry – nothing here is *yours*! (*Jocular, to* MARY.) Clinched *that* deal across this desk. Not one of my better ones, I'll admit. Her father definitely got the better end. She barely cost him a dime and she should have cost *a lot* to offload. Very plain. Hairy too. Look. And / no spring chicken either.

This runs off BETH – *she has had this recounted to her many times.*

BETH (*muttering*). No spring chicken –

HAL. You don't think I *earned* that money? I earned *all* the money around here and you are not getting one penny of it!

BETH. I don't want it. I have my jewels, Hal. Eighteen carats fastened round my throat every time you got caught screwing around. That's a whole lot of carats. That *I* earned. All tucked up safely in a downtown vault with my name on it.

HAL (*furious*). What, they got a vault down there with *Nurse Ratchett* on it?!!

Suddenly MARY *makes a desperate appeal to* HAL.

MARY. *Cash!* You could just give me some – !

BETH. Ha!

MARY. What?!

BETH. A rich man never has cash. No. The sum total of all the cash in this house is my fifty-dollar cab fare out of it. And you are not getting it.

MARY. No. No way. I don't believe that! I don't – (*To* HAL.) You *must* have – !

BETH. No. (*Pointing to the cheque.*) That's all you get from him. At least it has a pretty picture on it. The price of greed. Take it 'home' and frame it.

Beat.

Look at you. The girl who wouldn't stoop to a free ride. Till the limo pulled up. And now you have nothing. Nothing at all. But what I can give you.

HAL *suddenly gets very excited.*

HAL. Walk out of here with as much of this stuff as you can carry! (*Gesturing to a dark gilt-framed landscape.*) That painting alone's worth a couple of big ones. And here, take this. (*Pulls a Greek vase off the top of a box beside him.*) Ming, I'd say. And this – (*Pulls out a sculpture.*) That's a… (*Has no idea what it is.*) it's got to be worth something. Wouldn't be here if it wasn't.

He holds the sculpture out to MARY.

Take it. Take it!

Reluctantly MARY *takes the ugly lump.*

BETH. Yes. Take it. And here.

She pulls something else out of the box – the first thing that comes to hand – a silver samovar – and slams it down on the desk.

Take this. Take the lot. Clean us out. And I will call our insurers first thing in the morning who have it all catalogued and you will not dare attempt to sell one iota of it. You will just be left with nowhere to live and a load of useless trinkets!

MARY *is so frustrated she is on the verge of tears.*

HAL *is furious.*

HAL. You're

BETH. a cunt, Hal, but I don't think you're going to have to look at me much longer. (*Turning to* MARY.) Is he?

Beat.

MARY *shakes her head – back in* BETH*'s court.*

Good.

HAL (*fighting a spasm as well as his anger*). Noooooooooooo!

BETH. He needs another shot. That last one –

HAL. I don't WANT – !

BETH. And he needs a change. You stink, Hal.

HAL. No! I *forbid* her to – !

BETH. Behave yourself. Or she'll make you. You know she can.

HAL. Yeah. A regular little Bruce – ...

BETH *doesn't know the word.*

MARY. Lee.

BETH. See? She's getting the hang of things already.

She turns to MARY.

You've seen his full colours now. What you're really getting
in to. But he is still my husband and, crazy as it sounds, I
still care for him, and I want him properly cared *for*. I
appreciate that he may not always make the job easy, but you
are being more than fairly remunerated.

HAL (*in spasm*). *See?!* See *now*? I told you what your 'job'
really was! What you're *really* getting in to! Make me suffer
for fifteen more long and bitter, twisted years to make her
happy! Can you not see that?!

BETH. No one could see that, Hal. It's ludicrous.

HAL. Are you really going to execute her sentence for her?

BETH. How appreciated I have been. Of course I don't want to
make you suffer, Hal! All I've done for the last fifteen years
is try to stop you suffering, I'm leaving now because *I* can't
suffer any more.

She picks up her belongings to go.

HAL *is in the way of the door.*

Please move of my way.

HAL. Isn't that funny? That's exactly what I intend on doing. Moving-out-of-your-way.

He wheels clear of the door.

Off you trot then. Fast as your little hooves can carry you. (*To* MARY.) You.

MARY. Yes?

He wheels round to face her – his back deliberately to BETH.

HAL. Let's you and I get down to some *real* business. I have a suit.

BETH (*dreading the answer*). What suit?

HAL (*ignoring* BETH). In tissue. Savile Row. London England. You'll know it. Cut to hold a hundred pounds more of me but never mind, it's the only one for this job. My clincher suit. All my best deals were done in it. Or one the same. I want you to bathe me, shave me and get me into it. A haircut probably wouldn't go amiss either. Think you can handle that, nursey?

MARY *nods, waiting for it to make sense.*

HAL *leans back and surveys his kingdom once more.*

Yes. This is the room for it.

He gives his desk a tap.

This is the room all right. Die as you live. And that is the suit. I've been saving it.

MARY. For what?

BETH. His funeral.

MARY. What?

HAL *leans in.*

HAL. She's got a Walmart worth of drugs up there. And you hold the keys to the kingdom. Grind it all up. No lumps –

MARY. What?

HAL. Grind it up.

MARY. No!

HAL. I can't swallow it otherwise. All you have to do then is mix it with some nice warm milk and –

MARY (*horrified*). No –

BETH. Why would she do that?

MARY. I'm *not* do– !!!

BETH. Shut up. Why would she do that, Hal?!

Wheeling around.

HAL (*'innocently'*). Still here, my chitterling?

BETH. Why would she –

HAL. She would do that, Beth – for the *deeds*.

Beat.

She would do that, Beth, to *own* this house.

BETH. She might have been stupid once but I really doubt she's going to be that stupid again. (*To* MARY.) Those deeds? As worthless as the cheque. He'll renege.

HAL. Except here's the clever part. I won't be *around* to renege.

And he wheels round to MARY *again, drawing her into collusion.*

Trust won't be an issue for you this time. Trust me. We'll get everything all locked off for you first this time. Make it airtight. You call the shots. Bring in whoever you want. Lawyers, bank managers, Santa Claus, whoever you want. And we keep it simple. My instructions to lawyer –'Give Mary Davies this house. Outright. In perpetuity, title and deed. Just as soon as I am dead.' My instructions to Mary Davies – 'Make sure I'm dead quick.'

MARY. Jesus –

HAL. You get to move in, she gets to move out, I get to move on. Everybody happy. (*Grinning wide at* BETH.) Go on then. Go if you're going.

BETH *doesn't budge*.

MARY. No. No. You're not serious!

HAL. All this, all yours, for all time, and no me or her anywhere in it, just you and three very happy little boys.

BETH. Why would you do that, Hal?

HAL. To get you, Beth.

Beat.

BETH (*to* MARY). There's a pestle and mortar in the kitchen.

MARY. What?

BETH. She's not going to do it, Hal. And neither are you.

HAL. Sure she is.

MARY. No, I'm not!

HAL. Why not?

MARY. Because I'm not going to *kill* you!

HAL. Not even for a house?

MARY. No! I'm not going to kill you for a house!

HAL (*in a spitting rage*). Then I will make sure you kill yourself for it! That every minute you spend here is a lifetime spent in hell and three little boys rotting in it with you. I will degrade and debase you in front of them every day that you stay here and degrade me. For a house. I will spew out obscenities and shit at you in equal, generous measure and I will slowly but scrupulously turn you into that – (*Pointing at* BETH.) twisted lump of pumice over there whose place you take. (*With great relish*.) It will give me something to live for.

BETH. Just keep him sedated.

HAL *tics furiously.*

That's all she has to do, Hal.

HAL. All she has to do, Beth. Copy you. (*To* MARY.) Keep me topped up with knock-out juice the whole time so you can ram anything you want into me after that! Everybody with their vested interests in keeping Hal trucking till the great hallelujah but *I* want to bow out!

BETH. Do we really need the histrionics?

HAL. How many times have I asked you to stop?

BETH. Never, Hal.

HAL. Don't lie. I've done enough of this and you know it. How many times have I said that to her, that I want to stop, and still here I am – with a backside like Braille she has stuck me so many times with drugs I don't want!

BETH. Stop lying.

HAL. Lying? Really? (*To* MARY.) Even got you to do it, didn't she? Did I look to you like I wanted that shot?

MARY *looks appalled.*

DID I?

MARY. No.

BETH. Don't tell me you're buying this nonsense? (*Pause.*) I really am ashamed, Hal, that there were times when I couldn't look after you as well as I should have –

HAL. Force-feeding me while I was gagging – !

BETH. Oh, please –

HAL (*pulling on his saggy belly*). I got the best foie gras this side of the Waldorf right here!

BETH. I have a duty of care.

HAL. Not if I have divested you of it. How many times have I done that and *still* you –

BETH. Never.

HAL. Liar!

BETH. You're the liar, Hal.

HAL. And the drugs all kept upstairs where I can't get to them? Is that a lie?

BETH. For your own safety. That is common procedure in –

HAL. And every belt and shoelace and *matchstick* removed from this floor –

BETH. That's nonsense!

HAL. And every window nailed shut!

BETH. That's a –

HAL (*to* MARY). ARE THE WINDOWS NAILED SHUT?

MARY. Yes.

BETH. So they don't fall apart! Look at them!

HAL. And why, Beth? Why? So you can keep me alive to *punish me*!

BETH. This is low, Hal, even for you.

HAL (*to* MARY). Do you think I *want* to live like this? That Harold John Patten *wants* to live like this?! *The Behemoth?!* Only *she* wants it! Look at me! (*Holding up spasming arms.*) I'm long done! I lost the stomach for this a long time ago. And the asshole. Already leaked and squirted most of myself out of it – slowly turning myself to shit! All my spoils – the fat of the land – the best of everything – all turned to shit. Do you really think I want to wait around for the last of me to plop out? (*Pause.*) For *what*?! Her *satisfaction*?!

BETH *is upset.* HAL *is distressed and in a violent spasm.*

BETH. That is not fair, Hal.

HAL (*to* MARY). Do you think I want this?

MARY *shakes her head.*

I'm done. I'm a… carcass. Smell me.

Beat.

Smell me.

MARY *nods – she can smell him.*

Remains.

He collapses back into his chair in full awful spasm. They watch him a moment.

MARY *goes to him and kneels in front of him.*

Beat.

MARY (*kindly*). Do you want me to change you, Hal?

HAL *doesn't respond.*

BETH (*moved*). He needs to be sedated. This is cruel. And he needs his dosage upped. That last shot didn't –

MARY *stands square to her.*

Beat.

What?

Beat.

What? (*Exhausted.*) You don't really believe what he's saying? What sort of a ghoul do you think I am?

MARY. I don't know what anybody in this house would or wouldn't do.

She turns away from BETH and kneels in front of HAL again.

Hal? Do you *want* a shot?

No response.

Hal?

Her tone and gesture appears to soothe him. When the spasm passes he looks up at her.

HAL. No.

Beat.

No. Don't do that to me. Not for her.

Beat.

You know what I want.

MARY *shakes her head.*

MARY. No.

HAL. A small act of – …

MARY. No –

HAL. For a very big house.

Beat.

How else is this going to end?

Beat.

This is the only way now.

MARY *stands up slowly.*

MARY. I think I'm going to be sick.

BETH. Don't do this to her, Hal.

HAL *(gently)*. You're not going to be sick. You're going to be strong. For your – …

MARY. Boys.

HAL. It's *help*. You are helping a man who needs it and is asking for it. Not hurting anyone.

BETH. Figuratively speaking.

HAL *(to MARY)*. Not hurting anyone.

MARY *starts pacing.*

BETH. Hal –

HAL *(imploring)*. Beth. Please.

BETH. Stop this.

HAL. I know it's hard for you. Even after –

BETH. Hal –

MARY. I can't do it! No. No, I'm sorry. Let me give you a shot, Hal.

Frustration is driving another tic.

Please. I think that's a good idea. I think things might look better then. Different.

BETH. Yes, Hal.

Beat.

MARY (*blurting*). What if I get caught?!

They are all momentarily silenced. MARY by her shame, HAL and BETH by shock that she is actually contemplating it.

What happens to my children if I end up in jail?

HAL. Nobody goes to jail from the big boys' playground.

BETH (*to* MARY). 'Cept for little girls.

HAL (*to* MARY). We'll get my man Buchanan in here. He'll keep you straight. He can make anything look legit. Even managed to keep *me* out of the pokey several times.

MARY. You never killed anyone!

BETH. Huh.

MARY *drags a worried look from* BETH *to* HAL.

HAL. I took a few scalps along the way. Scalp or be scalped. But I think you're beginning to see that?

MARY (*reluctantly*). Yes.

HAL. And it's not like anyone's gonna be too surprised, is it? At me shuffling off? (*Pause.*) It'll even make plenty of people real happy.

Beat.

Me for one.

Beat.

MARY. Hal. Are you sure?

HAL. Yes.

MARY. Sure?

HAL. Yes. Fifteen years without a steak, a bourbon, a Cuban, an erection, a dry bed, just her, and this, and the likelihood of a lot more of it. I am sure.

Beat.

MARY (*quietly*). I can't do it.

HAL *explodes.*

HAL. What *are* you going to do then?! *Leave?*

BETH. She doesn't *have* to!

HAL. She's not staying if she's not / *useful*!

MARY. I CAN'T DO IT *THAT* WAY!

They both stop and stare at her.

The way you said. I can't do it *that* way.

BETH (*upset*). No. You're not going to do it *any* way.

HAL. Shush –

BETH. I can't bear this.

MARY (*quietly*). I think we should let him have what he wants.

BETH. What? There's no way I can let you do this! He's my *husband*!

HAL (*kindly*). Beth –

MARY. You don't want him.

BETH. But I don't want...!

MARY. He doesn't even want himself. I think we should let him have what he does want.

BETH. No!

MARY. Why not?!

BETH. *Because!!!* He's my husband.

HAL. You should go, Beth. It's okay. It's okay.

MARY. Yes.

BETH. It's not okay!

MARY. Yes. I am going to help him. Yes. I can do that. I think. In a way that people do – that's allowed. I think. A civilised way.

BETH. *Civilised?!* This is not –

MARY, *hardly believing the words that are coming out of her mouth, addresses* HAL.

MARY. I will make your food for you, every day, and bring it to you. And all your medicine and fluids and whatever else you need. I won't force anything into you, nothing, and if you don't want it, then you don't take it. If that is what you want. Do you understand?

BETH. He'll be in agony! Hal –

MARY (*ignoring her*). What I'm saying to you? Do you – ?

BETH (*getting more and more wound up*). He'll be in agony for *months*!

MARY. – And I'll be here with you and I'll keep you clean, and comfortable, and pain free. For the duration. Do you understand, Hal? That is what I will do.

BETH. The *duration*?! Disguise that any way you want – it's *murder*!

HAL. Deal.

BETH. *What?*

HAL. It's a clinch.

BETH. It's *murder*!

MARY (*exhausted*). It's not.

HAL (*gently*). It's not if I say it isn't. I say she is helping a dying man to a dignified death.

BETH. No!

HAL (*to calm her*). Elizabeth, I really think you should go now.

BETH *can't move*.

MARY. Yes.

Beat.

HAL. Go.

Beat.

For your own sake. Wherever it is you're going. It'll not take long. A few months at most.

BETH. Yes.

BETH *lets the door swing closed*.

(*Viciously*.) And that is not long enough.

Beat.

HAL. Check.

Beat.

HAL *is grinning*.

BETH (*calmly to* MARY). I could kill him myself. (*Pause*.) Except that he doesn't deserve to die.

MARY. What?

BETH. He deserves to have to live with himself.

Beat.

For what he did.

Beat.

Every last minute of that rank existence.

MARY. Oh my God, you *were* / keeping –

HAL. Shut up and listen.

Beat.

Go on, Beth. Tell her what I did.

BETH. He killed my son.

Beat.

MARY. What?

HAL. I killed her son. (*Facetiously.*) I knew there was a reason. (*To* BETH.) And how did I kill him?

Beat.

Tell her. Tell her how I killed him.

BETH *points at* HAL *in disgust.*

BETH. By giving him *that.*

HAL *nods.*

HAL (*holding out his spasming arms*). By giving him this. And so, here you are. Exacting your revenge. Tenfold. Like a demented Apache squaw. Aren't you?

BETH. Yes.

HAL *laughs.*

MARY. Jesus.

HAL (*to* MARY, *victorious*). And you thought I was making this shit up. No one could make this shit up. The things we do for John. (*To* BETH.) A genetic disease, Beth. An act of fate. A loaded dice. The dealer's – ...

BETH (*to* HAL). Not because you had it, Hal. Because you didn't tell me.

HAL (*well-worn territory*). I didn't know.

BETH (*to* MARY). He knew. He just didn't bother to tell me.

HAL. Why would I do that, Beth?

BETH. Same reason you do anything, Hal. For money.

HAL. What money?

Beat.

What money?

Beat.

Your *wedding endowment*? That *pittance*? Horseshit!

BETH. You should have told me.

HAL. I didn't know!

BETH. I'd have had a choice then. And I wouldn't have chosen THIS! But you wanted that money so you didn't tell me. You *sold* him. Him *and* me. For a pittance. For cash-flow problems. For some grubby deal only my father was desperate enough to touch. (*Lifting the samovar.*) My only child – not even worth that!

Beat.

HAL. You knew too.

BETH. I knew nothing! Nobody saw fit to tell me anything!

HAL. You knew. You saw my father. Heard about his. Same as everybody. You saw exactly what was coming down the line. You just chose not to see it. Cos you saw the money better.

BETH. What? No!

HAL. Especially after all of Daddy dearest's ships had sunk. You couldn't jump my gravy train fast enough. *Hoofed* your way up that aisle.

BETH. No! Stop –

HAL. Hoof. Hoof. Hoof. Hoof.

BETH. Stop –

HAL. Eyes straight ahead – fixed on all the lovely shiny pennies. Hoof hoof hoof. You sold him too, Beth.

BETH. Stop, Hal!

HAL. You just didn't think you'd ever have to pay the price, is that right? Isn't that right, Beth?

Beat.

BETH. But you were the one who gave it to him!

Beat.

HAL. Yes. Yes, I was. I knew and I gave it to him anyway. I thought, so what?

A series of tics build throughout this which HAL *tries to ignore.*

He'd be an old man when he got it and I'd be in my grave and I wouldn't have to see it, so so what? The way it's always been in this family. But I didn't know about that other kind – that... *infant* kind. That *juvenile* form. Didn't think I'd have to see a sick...

He holds his hand out to John's little height.

Seven years old. Didn't bet on that. Didn't think I'd have to *watch*. So punish me. But you dole it out. Because there are two of us in it. Me and you. You and me. And the things we do for John.

Beat.

(*To* MARY, *without taking his eyes off* BETH.) Your services are no longer required.

MARY (*dazed*). They're no longer on offer. I don't think there could be anything worse for me out there than in here.

HAL. Aren't you lucky. Now git.

MARY. Beth?

BETH *makes no acknowledgement.*

HAL. Git!

MARY (*hesitantly*). Beth? Could I just –

HAL (*turning to her*). Just what?! What?

MARY. Just... enough for gas? I don't have –

HAL. Get out.

MARY. Beth?

HAL. The Manhattan Pattens don't do philanthropy!

MARY. What?

HAL. What did you *do* for it?!

MARY. What?

HAL. You came in with nothing. You put nothing on the table. You leave with nothing.

BETH (*quietly, staring straight ahead of her*). Except you didn't see. Did you, Hal?

She raises her eyes to HAL.

Made sure you were always drunk or absent. Only came back when John was dead and you were too sick to get your dick or your drink in any of the right holes any more. Expecting me to forgive you, *nurse* you, tell you it wasn't your fault. There there –

HAL. Elizabeth. I knew exactly what you'd do to me. It's what I came home *for*. My penance. Every last long and bitter day of it. And you haven't let me down. Thank you. You're a horrible woman.

Beat.

What, you think I couldn't be dead by now if *that* was what I wanted?

MARY. You mean you put me through all that and you never even wanted me to – ?!

HAL. *I just wanted you to leave!* (*To* BETH.) But I knew if you thought I wanted a quick way out, *you'd* stay. To make sure there wasn't one. And I wanted you to stay.

Beat.

MARY. I'd've done the world a favour topping you.

HAL. Get out.

BETH. Stay where you are.

BETH stands, depleted.

Someone tells you every day that you're a horrible woman, and one day that's what you are. A horrible woman.

HAL. You were horrible when I met you. Sit down.

She picks up her handbag.

BETH. The things we do for John.

MARY. Beth –

BETH (*to* HAL). I don't care what happens to you now.

HAL. Sit down!

She heads for the door.

MARY. Beth –

BETH. I don't have change of fifty.

MARY. NO! WHERE ARE YOU *GOING*?!

BETH doesn't break her stride.

You can't just leave him here to die!

BETH. I'm not. You're here.

MARY. I'm not staying!

BETH (*her hand on the door*). Then it'll be you leaving him to die.

BETH exits.

HAL is all twisted up and groaning in anger and illness.

MARY. Shit!

MARY suddenly makes a dive after BETH and yanks her back into the room, pushing her down on to the floor.

Where's your wallet?

HAL relaxes somewhat with the sight of his wife back in the room.

MARY *grabs* BETH*'s bag –* BETH *doesn't let go of it.*

WHERE'S YOUR WALLET?!

BETH (*fighting hard*). Get off – !

MARY (*genuine*). I am really sorry, Beth, that it's ended up like this.

They wrestle over the bag.

But *twenty dollars*! Christ!

BETH. I only have a fifty! And I need it!

MARY. Give me the – (*Pulling.*)

HAL. Kitty really does like to play.

BETH. It's all I have! I need it!

MARY. I need it too!

HAL, *in his wheelie chair, travels to the chair that* MARY *vacated. Unseen by either woman, he lifts the keys she dropped there.*

MARY *wrenches the bag free.*

BETH. No, please!

BETH *gets* MARY *by the ankles, threatening to topple her.* MARY *pulls out the hammer and whacks it down hard on the floor very close to* BETH *with a violent crack.*

Everyone is silent and still.

Beat.

MARY (*calmly*). Now. Twenty dollars. Okay? And I'll send it back. That I promise. (*Sliding the hammer back in her belt.*) I wouldn't be in debt to you two for anything. (*Going through the bag.*) Where is your wallet?

MARY *rummages deep in the bag for the wallet – and she pulls out a black-velvet roll which unfurls to reveal several jewel-studded necklaces and strings of pearls.*

MARY*'s jaw drops*.

HAL *roars laughing*.

BETH. NO! NO!

HAL. Yes! Yes! Ha-ha! Some downtown vault you got there,
Beth! (*To* MARY, *jubilant*.) Run! Take it and run!

MARY *is frozen – staring at the riches*.

BETH. It's all I have. They're mine!

HAL. *I* bought them! They're mine!

BETH. They're *mine*! (*Pointing, desperate*.) That one was for
Lyla Boden, an actress with the clap!

HAL. It belongs to Mary Davies now!

BETH. And the diamond one?

HAL. Come on, rookie, bring home the bacon!

BETH. Diamonds for my *sister*. (*To* MARY.) You remember
that, Mary Davies. My *sister*!

MARY *can't bear to hold the filthy things any longer and all
frustration and fury, she flings the jewels on the ground*.

MARY. The fifty. I just want the fifty!

HAL. A lobotomy is what you want! Shit. *Murder* was no
problem ten minutes ago.

MARY. Fifty will get me out of here and that is all I want right
now! (*Turning to* HAL.) I think I earned fifty.

MARY *locates the wallet. She tears it open for the fifty, and
instead pulls out a huge wad of cash*.

Beat.

Christ.

HAL. Heh-heh-heh!

MARY *looks at* BETH.

MARY. *Twenty* dollars.

BETH is ashen.

If you had just given me twenty dollars!

Beat.

I'd've been happy. I'd've been gone.

She wraps her fist around the wad.

Would have been the best twenty dollars you ever spent in your life.

BETH (*weakly*). Please –

Beat.

MARY. Mary Davies doesn't do philanthropy.

MARY exits.

BETH watches the door swing closed, pushes the jewels away from her, and buries her head.

Footsteps thunder down the stairs.

The front door slams.

HAL goes to the window to watch.

Beat.

HAL. There she goes. Like the last of the Mohicans. No wonder they died out. (*Pause.*) You don't think she'll pay it back? (*Disgusted that she might.*)

He turns and looks at his wife on the floor.

Are you just going to stay there till you rot?

No answer.

Beat.

BETH. I didn't even want to leave till she came here.

HAL. I'm glad you didn't. I would miss you, my Betsy. All our cosy little chats.

Beat.

BETH. Now what am I going to do?

HAL. I have something for you.

He holds out the keys to the medicine cabinet.

Keys to the kingdom.

BETH *looks, but doesn't take them.*

These are yours. You take these.

She still doesn't take them.

He puts them round her neck.

And you do such a good job.

BETH *doesn't move.*

I'm really tired now. Want me to help you up to bed?

No response.

Sometimes I like to go up there and watch you sleep.

Beat.

BETH *comes to.*

BETH. What? No you don't. That's a lie. You can't...

HAL *shrugs.*

That is a lie.

You can't get up the stairs.

Beat.

HAL. Go to bed and see.

Beat.

Tomorrow is another day. Tomorrow is –

BETH*'s eyes travel down to the strings of jewellery in her hand, and a smile travels across her face.*

– another day. Tomorrow is –

BETH. A day I might not be here.

(*Fondling the jewellery.*) Tomorrow is – a day I might be gone.

HAL. You wouldn't.

Beat.

You wouldn't leave me here by myself?

BETH. Go to bed and see.

HAL *can't move.*

Slow fade on BETH's *smile.*

Blackout.

The End.

A Nick Hern Book

The House Keeper first published in Great Britain as a paperback original in 2012 by Nick Hern Books Limited, 14 Larden Road, London W3 7ST

The House Keeper copyright © 2012 Morna Regan

Morna Regan has asserted her right to be identified as the author of this work

Cover photograph by Pat Redmond
Cover design by Ned Hoste, 2H

Typeset by Nick Hern Books, London
Printed in the UK by Mimeo Ltd, Huntingdon, Cambridgeshire PE29 6XX

A CIP catalogue record for this book is available from the British Library

ISBN 978 1 84842 272 8